everward

A

POETRY

COLLECTION

EVERWARD

Cover illustration: "Journey Everward" by Rachel Murphy

Learn more about the author's journey at: www.journeyeverward.com

everward

ONE MAN'S JOURNEY THROUGH
DECLARATION, DISCOVERY & DISCERNMENT

A

POETRY

COLLECTION

W.G. KIRST

Special thanks to my pre-readers and editors of sorts:

Jeff, Paul, David, Jonathan, Dave, Lou, Pete, Rachel, Shawna, Donald, Stephen, Allison and many more.

Thank you to Rachel Murphy for the cover designs for this collection and trusting my words to serve as a canvas upon which we created together.

I chose this script

…to learn
…to teach
…to connect
…to thread
…to bridge
…to heal.

How do we curate? How do we hold? How do we tend?

Listen, attune, align.
You've been here before.
You'll be again.

It's all a puzzle.
Where shall we begin?

Your works, your words, your wisdom.
Don't be concerned that they are not seen.
Don't be dismayed that they are not heard.
Know that they will be felt when the timing is right, and the
signal is strong, and others have aligned to attune.

Note from the Author:

Poetry plays a critical role in my life. I can't think of a time when poetry and the power of words stitched together didn't somehow shape the way I see the world. Like a mosaic in a long-forgotten chapel, each word uniquely expressed is meant to be bathed in dusk's light for the greater collective.

From the first nursery rhyme I recited in my earliest days, to the captivating dimensions created by Khalil Gibran and Alexander Pushkin, words have always made worlds for me. And it is in these worlds I often seek a port of call.

As I listen to the creations and citations of writers and poets like Pádraig Ó Tuama and Jarod K. Anderson, the words serve as light illuminating an inner room and stirring a desire to reflect that light.

Poets are playdates for the brokenhearted. And their words serve to light the way toward healing. That is what the words in the following pages did for me. I can only hope you find them worthy as well.

Like any collection it could be described as eclectic and eccentric and somehow anchoring along the way. This collection of writing spans a few decades of work. Some were a stream of consciousness, others practically imprinted on a page where I found myself tracing letters that seemed to be there before I was aware, then erased a few times over. Phantom poetry some might say, like the cryptic Count St. Germain. I arrived at the belief that it all belongs and will find its way in its own time. And now it belongs to you.

It is hard to make a home without at least a few dozen books of poetry strewn about you. Where you rest, where you sleep, where you break bread and fill hallways with laughter…poetry lives, poetry breathes. Never more than a few steps and perhaps an arm's length away, is the infinite canvas of inspiration ready for you to delve and dive and detect the human heartbeat.

Form or free, it never really mattered to me. And now I set them free. I fear feeling phantom amidst the release. So, I release.

W.G. Kirst - August 8, 2023

"Whether it's 10 souls finding their ways to 10 meditation cushions or 10 butterflies finding their way to 10,000 petals, mapmaking is a mysterious process, and the process doesn't visually map to what we are creating."

- W.G. Kirst

Contents

Part 1: I will...I am

...dance/...healing

49 steps taken, one lost from longing
Love appears an eternal sentence for those struggling to breathe
Yearning for touch, afraid of affection
Cold steel can't be a cage when its wielding in your hands
Hot steel hits the floor, shatters the pane on which we once danced
The trigger falls, the treble clangs to a bass beat abandoned
Stage less, breathless, no longer fearless
Is that my heartbeat or the downbeat?
My ears are ringing, my friends are screaming
Is that popping or clapping
Last words, last texts, lasting thoughts
In certainty came sanctuary
Hold each other, let go together
Fight for one more break together until its over
I will dance...I am healing
You're joy, your spontaneity, your beauty, your passion
None of these are gone – it's in all of us who celebrate
I feel them all around me every time the wind brushes my face
And brings a smile

...renew/...remembering

What may mark the end of an era
A parting glass, a passing storm, a folded flag
There is no final note to tap where there was always music
Even till the end
A bar to hum and hold on to, a melody to let go and dance in
Step it out for Mary
A last breath is gasped, a last sun is set, a Bastille sentence ends
Your *lettres de cachet* burn to ashes, your trial is now over
Where a king may be released from the laws
We are bound by Claddagh, all High Kings and clans of Ireland
A curse of diffidence while reaching
Where renewal comes in remembering
Wind swept, salt kissed, and sun soaked
Bless the moments and the ages

...relent/...rising

Destination in transaction
Perspective bagged and tagged "priceless"
Anticipation arrival with curbside pick up of trepidation
Screening...securing...gripping...lifting...breathing
Fingertip technology and basic psychology
In A and B for me to see and cling to occasionally
From transaction to ascension...journeys are data and desire
10,000 reasons to find comfort in between the 1s and 0s
Steps I control, feet I do not...observe what's real and is now
Levels clear, breaths steady, chimes indicate it is safe to smile
Symphonies of progress and power and perspective
Play to move me from six wheels to silver wings
To sky kissed snow caps rows of minds wander
I began to ponder "next best action"
My soul will bounce, and my heart will strain to hold things still
And through life's down drafts I will relent and remember
I am rising

...mourn/...weeping

The arc only becomes itself
When one half dips and falls
No more thinking this journey
From down this low, has only up to go
Face the Earth, closing out, breathing in
Finding two points across two planes
Tonal, polar, distant, divergent
Where balance strives, it seldom thrives
One strand stands to earn
The other seeks a voice to learn
From within, the what, the how
To be aware, and for once allow
Myself to mourn and then to weep
It's not what you take, but what you keep
What is calling, crying, falling, living

...reveal/...happy

Countdown to a new beginning
Years in the waiting
Tears in the making
From 20 to 21, where in a number
Lies a newfound freedom
It's my time in town
This night will go down in history
My journey, your trials, our triumph
I will reveal I am happy
Start with a snapshot of this moment
I'm on the edge of my potential
My passion, my glory
Together we will tell our story
So no one forgets
The silent heroes accused only of love
Years of building fortresses
Hasn't made us stronger
But gave us the bonds
To live a life of love together
And freedom even longer

...embark/...unafraid

1 and 1 and 1 in the same
This will be the year to celebrate
To breathe easy, walk lighter, stand taller
No longer will my chin snap to my shoulder
To glance back, wince and maybe wonder
Instead I will snap to and straighten my cover
The road less marched just got clearer
Because you can only see footprints now
Will you follow or will you filter you out
Progress and pain are just a path apart
Playing by the rules no longer makes the cut
But are you man enough to step up?

...sing/...thankful

You accompanied me on this journey
And I never had to
Like a fellow traveler you joined me
At every station I'd ride and you'd write
And through 1s and 0s of technostalgia
By way of the world's smallest drum
I counted you in and we kept this bearable
And so I say Amen to Levi's cries
Cause I am one of the ones ivory has the power to save
And whoever is playing God to me, save it
Because there will be no more lies
I saw this outloud and out of respect, pour amour
Like Williams' fiery red crown, I've let the flames begin
And even though I don't want to be your hero
It is my turn to be brave
And since there is no day but today
Do I need to answer or do I let it ride?
And there's ever tension and a spark
In the gravity I choose to defy
Because there's only one Juliet in this alibi

...announce/...landing

Tonight I touch down
A different man and I extend a hand
To the way it should have been, back then
I can't buy back the time, but I will certainly try
It's true I may never have tired
Never would have dropped my guard
Nor the arm that kept you at bay
But it's no longer my game to play
And what if today is your last day
Then what? Is this really how you want it to be?
Do you half care if it's a she or a he?
As long as you know I'm free
To see, to be, to love, to share in memory
Cheers to humanity, raise your glass
Whose rules are these anyway?

...tell you/...happy

Today, finally, my everywhen
I will tell you...I am happy
Stumbling upon happiness
Has been quite a journey
You may read it by paragraph
Or even line by line
But look in between
You see them as gaps, to me they shine
The world feels lighter today
And I can ask Atlas, is this how it feels to shrug?
One more hour
One short drive
Across the river to the mild, mild west
I take one more breath, I can do this
Here I go
3-2-1
Ctrl+Alt+DEL

Part 2: Grief is a Teacher

The Ones We Carry In Love

Every expression of love
Means embracing the edge
Of something that wasn't there before
And won't be there in the after
In the sorrows there where we find the commons
But we do not allow ourselves to arrive
With our bundle of gifts, offerings
Because we are tired from our journey
Of tending all that is tender and heavy
The terrain is unfamiliar and familial
All at once, so which way do I turn?
Which passageway do I take?
Which light do I shine?
My compass spins North, East, South, West
Taking me in circles
I guess the only place left to go
Is down...inside...deep...beyond

Through Our Tears the World Appears

Through our tears the world appears blurry
And through our tears the cleansing of our gaze occurs
What might we see now?
She calls to me as I sonder
"Let the water hold you, like I can no longer
For you will always find me in the waves"
Count our time in tides, it's a siren's song Poseidon craves
Father of Time tied to daughter of Earth, a titanic armored heart
Is this the grip of grief, or the devouring and comforting
Handholding of heartbreak
I guess grief is like fissures, those cuts in the Earth
To allow pressure to release
And lyrics are lineage to the boy who got lost long ago
Among the claps and shouts and clangs of armor
Limb by limb, tether and tree, suspended in the ethereal
And the in between where serpents slither
And bears abound and shrunken look from beyond the heavens
To nurse the wound

The No Letter Language

Grief is a language
But there's no alphabet to memorize
No character to trace
No sounds to mimic
Only feelings immutable can we study
In complete darkness
Stillness, silence
In this cave can we draw the language
And where there's light, our abilities to understand fade
Darkness is the grammar
Silence is the preposition
Stillness is the diction
The blindfold is the chisel
The nightmask is a stencil
Waves bring movement
Make cracks appear
Shade in the caverns and the nautilus
Leave the darkest chambers fresh and clear

Searching for the Formless

An inspirational conversation reminds me
Searching for the formless is a lifelong journey
It has so much to teach us
It often starts with letting go
Find happiness in the movement alone
And you'll discover your where
This destination is unknown
Grief is a river.
Always in motion and an ever present invitation
To submerge in the restless flow of life

My Travertine Heart

Deposited by a spring of eternal love
A terminal fibrous heart muscle strains
Blocked aqueducts still gave our tribe a stream
Trickling like rapid rainfall from my eyes
Taming of the waters amidst an ocean's emotion
The eldest titan bridled Hippocampus' gallop
Capricornus strength in the first and the tenth
Even your smallest wisdom waterfalls
Disturb the surface fluids of this chalice
Like a coin tossed into a river a shining salve
My ribs break under the pressure of this cup
Missing commune and absent rituals
Insufficient drama in this urban mess
Where do I address the buildings of expectation
Where is the boundary stone of Corinth
Where is the alter of lapis over my spirit
I follow the pathways and chambers and melodies
That lead me to the junction of your late tributary
To ride the currents of confluence to Atlantis

Hold the Door

The air is cleaner, pure, crisp
So why is it so hard to breathe?
The noise abated, the silence invited
So why is it so hard to listen to the body?

The body slows, the mind races
So why is it so hard to feel?
The eyes read, the ears listen
So why is it so hard to understand?

How does one hold the door
But not touch the door?
How do we hold one another
But on the other side of the street?

How do we shelter
In place of community?
How do we commune
On what's common?

Among us, amidst us, between us
In redrawing a reality, are we re-membering our humanity?
We are tested and resistant
Do you feel the resonance at its height, 3am?

Is this resilient relating we spoke of
And still never said a word?
We learn, we yearn
And the light show above us takes another turn

Take to rest from overwhelm
Empathy is power, compassion is connection
Open, join, click, connect
And uncover, discover, another in you

The way through, we've become new
When will I see you?

An Echo's Embrace

Packing for a car ride
Early fall morning
Sadness in the air
Sense of growing at each mile passed
Heartbeats of hesitation
Feeling the faith of another there with you
Distant echoes of embraces

Tethers

The candles are tethers
Where the light dances I'll be
We were never built for forevers
I'll be there when you need, just ask me

Stillpoint

Slowing...
To a stillpoint
One breath being held by us
It's a graduation for us
Wise ones

Disdain

What would it take for us to be whole again?
I assured you that nothing would replace
I wanted you to believe me, pretend
But you could no longer look me in the face
Your every glance renewed it, man's disgrace
The earth shifted below me as I stood
No longer united, she said, "you're good"
A chasm formed for me to fall inside
The sun sets, a son sets his pride aside
This boat has no sails, trust her to the tide

Marginalia of Loss

Don't walk on white carpet
You know you're going to spill
Over the sea wall comes the surge
Of emotions and the sound of the ocean
Call to me like an octopus teacher
Return to school for these daily lessons
With Pandora's syllabus to set the course
Thumb up to take this ride
Though the tides tell me I'm against all odds
There's a waiting room I must be admitted
Or leave me here, to hold the space my body needs
Symbolism of the in between
The liminal
The marginalia of loss

Pandemica

Invite to reflection the gift of pandemica
Invite to reflection the gift of pandemica
Everything is up for consideration and dissolution
Everything is up for consideration and dissolution
Everything is pandemica and reflection
To invite up the gift of consideration dissolution

Reflect on the origins of our engagement
Reflect on the origins of our engagement
Seek wisdom in the edifice while you can
Seek wisdom in the edifice while you can
Edifice of engagement while our origins
Reflect wisdom, you can seek

How are their patterns in the beautiful
How are their patterns in the beautiful
What are the virtues as a person
What are the virtues as a person
Beautiful virtues are how a person
Patterns as the are in their what

Invite the patterns of a person in dissolution
Up the consideration, how engagement and reflection are
everything
Seek our origins of pandemica, while you can
What gift to a beautiful edifice, reflect as the virtues are wisdom

Penelope's Stitches

What is the fear that guides my ship
In the direction of what is said to be
Certain, you say, the guise of authority
The endless stitching of Penelope

Storms will form, tides will swell
Ulysses cast his own shackled spell
Winds carry you back to where you fell
The three tongs of Triton make a prison cell

Close my eyes to see in this cave
Firelight dances between those we save
Let it not blind my mind's eye
The stake I carry, the monster's stave

How can I conceal from the world my call
And keep dancing on this Titan's wall
Where is the mentor atlas for my ellipsis
To come home to the wisdom in us all

Part 3: Planet Waking

No Snooze Button

Planet waking has no snooze button
You can't send a light year call to voicemail
Are you ready to answer the call?
And when you are finally in the spotlight
The question arises…
Do you perform the dance moves that people expect
To keep the light on you or do you risk your authentic movement
Even if it means risking sudden darkness on the stage
At this stage
Take to the diving board
To soar requires abandon
Poolsides, tide pools, and shallow safety zones bring knowing
But you're here to go beyond what the world knows of us
To show us…we can each trust our own clock of connection

Time

My mind may understand the 2D world
And society's desire to plot...things
On a simple X,Y axis
But my heart simply cannot find
Its place on this limited plane
It continues to soar and rise and wander to where
It is called and where it has the most impact
That place is uncharted still
What do you say? Shall we go? Shall we venture?
Shall we redraw the dimensions of perception and deception?
What are canyons if not energetic superhighways of spiritual
meditation?
What are puddles if not reflection of moments of joy?
What are pools if not collections of our consciousness?
Your cells are in a stage of perfection by nature
Fifty trillion cells can't be wrong and still we deceive ourselves with a
timepiece
Telling us we can't achieve inner peace because there's not enough
time

Sleeping In

There is a sense of stillness in me, finally
This activist heart, the Veteran mind knows no peace
But it feels like sleeping in today
Grabbing those final moments of womb-like respite
Fetal position, back to the waters, pulling the covers up
Take cover! Over your shoulder, you yell, a signal
A figure, suddenly you see your grandmother
She's here to tuck you in, like a flag draped coffin
Her covers made of hundreds of wildflowers
Laid around a fountain, candle wax dripped and dried
Tears and chalk epitaphs and birthdays stolen in the night
Soul pain, hunger strikes, writing circles with time running out
Breaths break the silence of the park, it's time to stretch fiercely
Time to yell it out as you find your feet again
Standing on a patchwork quilt folded neatly on display
For all to see and for all to seize the day
What are those things given, granted, gifted, offered in freedom
Blades of grass dance in the solstice winds
A zephyr stirs in the hearts of those who pass through here
Echo the enchanted for all of you to follow
You may not be able to see me through the crowds
But I can see you
You may not be able to hear me through the cries
But I can hear you.
You may not be able to feel me through the rumbles
But I can feel you.
I'll take the overwatch as others are sleeping in.

Tendency & Tenderness

There's a human tendency to want to know
But it's in the waiting and the tension where we most grow
"How long is the wait?" they ask the hostess, doctor and doula
"Four years" you reply from the discomfort of the crowd
In that time, think how much we know and grow
Plant the seeds of hope our mothers gave
Watch them grow with love and care
As you're thrown out of line and you align
Here's to a better together...if you even dare
The answers feel like prisons
The questions a warm pool of healing waters
I feel pressure to accelerate and decelerate
All at once

A Figment of Pontifex

My hands flow over the rocks that once tumbled
From what's left of a phantom volcano, each the breath of Hades
The winds race like a chariot around the circus of her peak
The haunting sounds of a chrysalis' song
The crackling, snapping, stretching, popping
In and out of my consciousness
Man's compass comes to a resting place
The ore beneath me finally grows still
Subsumed, subduction, seduction reigns
In bishoprics and buttresses gold sustains, gems cut
Sabine spades pierce me, spills fill, sanguine painted current
Red runs the Rubicon
And swirls of shame fixed this ancient game
The trinity, troikas and pyramids fall all around me
The sons of Horus cry as storms fill the sky
The day after paternal placebo phantoms parade
Palatine Hill where chants and chariots once rose, now haunt
Help me fall, like the 36 spears from the skies of Jupiter
August, us everward seeking bridge back to the estuaries
I was good all along
The waters were pure all along

We Fight the Autofill

Isn't every entry a tug of war with a wiser machine
Suggestions are supposed to be shaping
But it feels like it is just excavating...eviscerating
Me if not for my words, my purest thoughts unheard
Then who am I left to be in the sea of soliloquy
When I say my everwhen, I mean my everwhen
Don't force your wheres and days on me
So suggestively, surreptitiously, lazily...will we ever see
I fight
I choose to fight
Every tap I zap that floating x keeps coming back
Those greyed out letters tease me, seducing me
Like the coming of a familiar song on the list that plays you
Hovering, saying wouldn't it just be easy to let me complete thee
I am not here to teach the lifeless, envisioning idea of silica
To speak for me is to truncate me
Efficiency be damned, it's suffocating who we are
Who we strive and strain to be...free
Fight the autocorrect, fuck your autofill
We are too complex and ought to be completed
Mostly by the stars and layers long since deleted

The Fallen Gaul

Twelve hundred twenty seven hours
My ring tells me that's how long we've slept together
This half year, feels like its gone on forever
So why try when I can't remember my own powers?
This blanket's a shield holding me up...against it all
Every time I shut my eyes, you see through my wall
The fallen Gaul faces the arms
Freed and frail battle cries, an age old tale
Let him be
Let him see
The coat stripped of me
Fathom for the tired
For every move misfired
The torc rope tightens around my enraged ego
I spiral in the sound that travels around
The chambers of heart now broken
I don't consent to those conquests
At the behest of the heads that now rest
Banners burn, words like pikes impale
A silent stirring
An uprising will prevail

Temperance of Ramses

Stop striving for perfection
Put down the bottle
You overlook the interim
You miss the mystery
Let us be your overwatch
While you're busy being
And delight us
No, unite us
By all your own doing
Seeing what you see
Not what you're told to be
Seeing with the heart
Sense the landscape
And what it means to be free
Exit Ramses' ramp and behold
The waters that hold us back
Sacred sons, sister moons
Revolutions of this rock a refuge
In movement even the tender shakes
Even in the darkness, my heart quakes
Exhaustion is a drum skin stretched taught
I am enough with new eyes and deep roots
Temperance is a dance who steps you know
So what do you say?
Shall we give it a go?

Awoken Within

The journey began
When I was awoken by a star
I didn't know it then
But my journey would lead me on a search
For who I am
Along the way I experienced growth
I encountered glances of the galactic
I chose to listen inward, everward
As a result, I lost the script
I gained my words
When I reached my destination
I learned all I need to know
Resides within
Because of my journey
I know I will write the stories
That need to be told
I trust the deepening
Of our journeys

Irish Drum

May I help you find the beat
To flap your wings to
If I fly too far and high
How will I hear you?
I could come to life again
On your skin
Jumping and leaping
Or could you help me whisper
My longings, my wishes
To go back
Into a time of softening
A time before my time
To see where the shame set in
And wander
A third way
Where intimacy can have a place
And plenty of space
The questions and challenges arise
Around forgiveness
And where love gets the last word

Response

It is in the ability to respond
That makes us responsible
It is in the habitual
That become betrayal
Guilt is the movement
Of the instinctual
Where frustrations end
New ideas begin
Be patient
Give it time
Most new ways bring discomfort
Without permission
We imprison ourselves
Completely open and closely held
What do we have to offer
At the sound of the bell?

Nine Waves In

Aim high your berm
Far beyond your domain shall cast
From this stance you carry the scales
And join long lines of ancestors
Up stairs you see your kin
And pass to them the scales
As you descend with ease and love

Market in Lviv

Orange stand bright against gray
Always and forever gray
Wondering how far this fruit journeys
To arrive here
Mandarin oranges worthy of a sign
Over zealous crowds gather around
The urge to buy is not here for me
I watch as generations behave
Differently around these bright colors
Will these be here tomorrow
Are these for their grandchildren
Will they sell them on the sidewalk
Tomorrow begins another day
Another gray day, a somber day
But a day where they face it
The three tips of the triton entice
Give hope to look, look for a way
Last trip? No, not now

Four Streams of Heartbreak

To write you have to put the baby down
But my being knows only its contractions and expansions
Invisible, illegible and inaudible
To an other, any other, other than me
My imprint, my heartprint
I fear this fusing is cut short
Don't cut the chord
I feel safe when I can see
Someone's heart
Revealed or concealed
I want to feel the fibrous threads
Of another's essence and being
I know duality dissipates
And we keep each other safe

The Many Faces of Lugh

Two faces sleep, a little longer, like the Sun
While another duality in me battles on
It's begun, the exchange of who they expect
To who they respect, and again, who I neglect
And what of oath and truth and tribe
A long hand can fight, and rule, and craft
And the long touch of a hand can also save a life
Where does a vow belong amidst the bending of our time
Is she sewn or forged or sheathed or bound
The five points where we gather, climb, battle and mourn
From our great towers, they too must fall, around us
For how can we learn where we must go, and what's to know
Unless we let the ripened fruit spill, to show us what's still to grow

St. Stephen's Green

The light dances through the leaves
On St. Stephen's Green
There's a quiver of a lip
There's the laughter of a child
The sound of splashing...a swan

Demarcation lines and defending with triggers
A gazebo brings them around again
You can't see them then?
Well, you must feel them, certainly

What paths we take around the green
Which bridge connects us to the space
The space between us all...you see it?
She does, I'm sure of it. Her smile tells me so

Three times around and a few crosses between
A temporal and timeless trinity
Entangled, wounded, found again
And carried. Finally carried.

Nine

What if the count begins with nine?
What if there are more dimensions
Then we see, feel, hold in a cube?
What if in this wave that's holding me
Is the boundary stone to the galactic?
As the shaman glimmers to the interstellar
His gaze tethering me to infinity
Isn't it just the other side of me?
To who does this storyline belong?
We cry to an unfinished song
Ride the thermals, flap no wings
See the unseen be the in between
We are uncharted and have been here before
Dis-cover, breathe for another
Glimpse to the lives of two brothers
Laughter, light, life awaits us
On this side of the barn door
And that breath was your own
In a plane you've never known

Mirrored Divinity

What would it feel like to live defiantly in delight?
So much defies us, a tree moth disguises
Part of the bark and then suddenly surprises
When it moves and flies away...what is today?
Dance of breath between surprise and delight
There is a bit of laughter before the night
What is laughter but a radical delight?

Pontifex & Pace

Peace is a bridge that must be built
Peace sits just behind the eyelids
Peace resides just beneath the sternum
Peace sprouts just below a touchpoint
Peace echoes just inside the canal
Peace sits just beyond where you're rooted

Find peace all around you
It exists in all of you.

Be in the world
Not of the world.

Shamrock

A powerful symbol
An imperfect trinity
All in one you are to many
Your edges imperfect
Reflective wounds
On the land
On the tribes the flock
And still you serve as a beacon
To represent creating
Calling, collecting
Is each a petal or platform
Are you a troika of hearts
Connecting together
By a central fiber
Are you as powerful in place
Or do you take on new life uprooted
Severed and snapped into a new fate
Thankful for the reminder of life

When Water Shakes

When the water shakes
I know it is signaling to me
I know it's intuition coming in
A way friendly and free

Streams interrupted opens my heart
For ease of integration and flow
Between these spaces and places
In the liminal there is joy

Vibrations, reverb, tremors and beats
Tell me to stop and take it in
It's when my signal is strengthened
It's when I listen to the unsound, unsaid

I ionize the molecules that shower me
And let them nourish me, encourage me
Re-member me, re-energize me
A love explosion

New Steps

Points of stillness
Stones that call us to them
Frequency is found if you feel first
What calls you in this life
What are you called in this life
To question is to take new step
To open is to acknowledge
To channel is to unfreeze a wave
Because energy is truth in movement
It will adapt and include
It may construct in growth
It will dance in and out of phase
We are resounding truth
Once born to be shared

Journey to Nourishment

I wonder how far you've traveled to me
I wonder who gave you your first dew in thirst
I wonder the feel of the soil that cradled you
And the hands that cultivated you to here

Do I get a chance to hold those hands someday
To place them over my heart, which swirls
And beats to frequency of the Earth
That pleasantly pulses through my canals and caverns

Movement may I never forsake you
Movement may you take me to savory
Movement may you slow me to know energy
Movement may you bring me to wonderment

Indigo

Deep indigo, almost purple
Why do you call
You find your way into my heath, alone
Slipstream into consciousness
Paint me the pleasure of potent patience
Powerful pronounced protocol like
The agenda is changing
You are fading
Into a seafoam of greener meadows
I find you in a wildflower
And in your bulbs
The doorways to the Cosmos
Your stars are seeds, her seeds are stars
A nest am I in
Masteam, where are you?
Tasmean you take your steps for us all
An steam carries the essence of our hope
Land somewhere
Dampen something
Replenish the seed and Earth

Shields Sprouting

Waterfalls of gratitude splash amidst me
Every drop contains a story
Every basin in a cauldron of nourishment
To keep the bones dancing, standing, typing

I reach out to Gaia and Sophia
Can she hear me?
She can feel me, this I know
Eye on eyes, I ionize every droplet to return
To source, to the delta and basin of this life

May you fall to reach the call of the parched
And the fields and the blood soaked shields
That need your quench, fall through my hands
Until we can dance
For that long, needed, overdue embrace of my heart

Find the roots, pour through the soil
Nurture the growth we can't see yet
You draw our goodness out of us
And sprout our heart's abundances

Atmos, Meet Cosmos

Listen for the pops, the clicks, the dust and the grit
It is in the grooves where we are granted the depth to dance
Unreality starts to set in when well-formed nuggets of knowledge
visit you
Like the elusively illusory pollinator
Suspending itself alongside your disbelief
Grief is the last act of love we can give to those we loved
Where there is deep grief, there was great love
Grief changes your address book
Grateful for the stories that capture the heart of a man
Invisibly written in the margins

Ribcage

Reflecting on the dance
The closeness of a prideful namesake gaze
Hands around my ribcage
Closeness, touch, less than a second
Before I am thrown into the air
Loving gaze broken
As I shatter the surface
Of the water that swallows me
The water, it never stops touching me
It never tires of holding me
My tears are incorporated and integrated
And appreciated in the waters
Elemental, parental, patriarchal

Elliott and His Friends

At the base of the spine
Cradles me the seat of the bike
More than it holds me
A tether is released
I don't need to fall
But I do
To feel the hand that made me
To heal me
This bike, this ship will hold me
Free me, heal me
I believe even though they say no
I run, I bike, I escape
As the pedals push me away
I think of Elliott and his friends
I want to fly over authority
And hear the ricochet of our laughter
Echo off the cul-de-sac below
There are truths unseen
I will never let you go

Call & Response

So says the crow
Every line of me its perfect length
Necessary for the wind to dance
Over it to lift
Matted close to my roots
Cleaner at my edges
I am hidden when attached
I am exposed when removed
I am fallen
Mine is now a different call.
Yours a delicate response
I feel like holding you delicately
Despite you giving me strength
Is that strange?
I must tell you
Your kin have helped me
We talk sometimes
When I wonder, I hear a call
And a response comes
But never in words
Only the crows know

Pain in the Fifth Digit

Pain in the fifth digit
Saturn spins
A baby's hand grasps the wings of manta rays
Mustangs race
Stars burst, no fault of mine
Stare into the flames, you fade away
When the world falls, the world falls in me
A cavernous gaze of sadness
Where one's third eye may be the North Star
Speckled space dust, patterns made
Hilltops of Cosmos, where do I stand
Feel it throw you into the wind
Still there's room for anyone
Vines are souls breeching
Lions mane meets the nights skies
Celestial incense arises green with envy
You know the reel before you
Chambers are meant for escape, or is it protection?
A six-sided gem stares at me in descent
Siblings join in a cavalry of horses pulling chariots
A hand reaches out balancing the red dawn
And in the blue gem there is always balance

Radar Station

Radar abandoned
I was told it was time to go
"Leave it all behind" they said
For where to I do not know
"The signal never failed" I pleaded
"Let me stay, I'll find a way"
Rejected, disrupted, corrupted
Their claims, such games people play
Snow drifts, water puddles, paint peels
May this body never forget
How it feels to come back one day
I've returned to the radar station
Its signal I've attuned, aligned alone
I can't say what it's telling us
I feel it in the bones

The Marauder's Mirror

Resist the urge to hit "Submit"
Don't cut the chord so soon
Sling the child in front of you
And move, just keep moving

The Drum and Feather

The Irish drum and far away feather
The drum asks the feather
Can I help you find a beat
To flap your wings to
The feather is needed to fly
To fly is needed to survive
The Irish drum is asking spirit
Can we help you feel your heartbeat
For it is matted down at its root
The crow's feather fears
If he flies too high and far
He will not be able to hear the beat
And lose the ability to fly
The crow's feather is telling me
Not to venture so far and so high
In achieving, doing, fulfilling
For I will lose the ability
To hear my heartbeat
And I will fall
The crow's feather says I could come down
And come to life again jumping on the goat's skin.

Shadows

Sitting on a beach the sun as my crown
The rays warm my heart and blind my eyes
The stinging of my past turns me around
Darkening each grain of sand there lies

Always with me, never is me
Darkening every grain of sand
It is my past from what I see
Unreachable by my hand
Impossible I know, but life will show
I leave shadows everywhere I go

Like spotlight to a star you follow me
Illuminating all that I show
But without you there just who will I be
Alone I turn and see my shadow

Cathedrals

Cathedrals of contemplation
Imagine what could be created
Cathedrals of compassion
Feel into all that could be healed
Cathedrals of creativity
Imagine what we could manifest
Invent, ignite

Shards of glass and stone cease to be
A pile of uncollectables when somebody
Contemplates it with the idea
Of a mosaic in the mind

Here's to the shards and stone
And oceans smoothed glass
That reflects our journey
May they pick us up once in a while

Starting Small

Before you can leap
You step

Before you can scale
You reach

Before you can summit
You surrender

Wildflowers don't know they are wild

We don't know we are throttled

Until we step among
All that is free and flowing and fragrant
To feel the foraging spirit

Your 74th Birthday

Every raindrop has a story
Does that story come to an end when it lands
Or simply trickle into another's story
A window is no longer a pane of glass
Now 1000 stories

End this night and start the day
With a thank you sent one's way
It is grounding and reaching
It is our founding and our teaching

Type one sentence, take one walk
Bring people together, share a vision
Teach at every turn and do good always
Gestures matter...we show up, no matter what

Gathering of Voices

What is consciousness but a gathering of voices
Unsolicited, unincumbered, unthoughtful
Don't see external validation, look inside
Reach inward and create clarity beside

Fear is a wave to evanesce
Less propagation the further it spans
And then it is the horizon
Where the sun kisses your forehead

But why challenge yourself with something
When we are always changing
When every step is a first step
In a universe that is shaping us outward

Stillness of Listening

Stillness is about listening
When you really listen you're hearing
A voice that is wiser than yourself
It is sure to be wiser than I am

So, listen. Just listen.
What are you inside?
Are you afraid that something will hit
A chord that you may never forget?

Gather, help, offer, laugh, listen
Connect and remember
We don't have to be alone
Just because our experience is singular
In nature

What is PRIDE?

You call it a month, I call it a movement
Some see a party, others a riot
What does it mean to commemorate, to liberate and to DEBATE?
Hand me the megaphone, I've got something to state
There are brothers and sisters dying alone, still today
So why are we arguing over the birthplace of gay?
Your block, my block, our home, these hearts
Historic heartbreak, just like love, never fades
Legal judgements alone won't save the day
Because in some States you cannot be born this way
Political or corporate, individual or collective, protest or rave
Local, national, global, don't tell ME how to behave
In the year 1978, on this very day, hands raised
The rainbow flag in the San Franciso Gay Freedom Day Parade
Let us not forget how far we've come
And how much there is to be done
When the unjust no longer reigns, and every heart is full of light
Only then will I close my eyes and rest, truly rest, with fear out of sight

The Poet's Pen

May you pick up the poet's pen
With the grip of what you hold and highlight
To finish the Forgotten Song
A chariot pointed North
A spider rounds a corner
A cloak drapes a mother protecting a child
A submarine lurks
A number 9 pencil writes the tests
Allowing me to mark my way

Scriptscrapers

Write the words that come to you in the liminal
For those are uncontaminated
And free of mental binds of a universe
Of so called scribes and scriptscrapers

Who have we become?
How far have we gone
When rest is considered revolutionary?

The jagged edges of forever
Stamp an origin story
For all to see and scan
Would this have felt easier at 32?

Find happiness in the movement alone
And you'll discover you
Once again...in the end
Where the destination is unknown

Epilogue

Story and poems and song are the chosen shield of the resistance, the rebels, the renegades. Woven together, words serve as a safeguard to those who never want to forget, and will not live in fear.

The chants and song, no man can imprison. You can raise the land, you can flood the valleys, you can burn the fields, but like the Sacred Earth has shown us, seeds, like stories, will grow again.

The cathedral of sky and sea and soil is where words will find her echo. Surely, you have heard the echo before. In a canyon? Across a lake? Above a waterfall or in a wood?

The Carmina Gadelica speak to me so delicately to swaddle me even now as I witness fires put out only by snowfalls, moths shrinking in size, just like the icecaps. Should we not elevate the words of the Ancients to remind us all we do not know...still? Do not our healings come from the Earth?

I was told as a child, there's no wound or scrape or scar the tears of the Earth could not heal. And so, I spent much time in our oceans, bathing in her tears. Only where do I put my tears now if I want to heal her in return?

I sit under a new moon in Capricorn and bend my knee in reflection... no, it's more a genuflection. And I am marked a Pagan for this gesture? And what of sun worship then? And the study of the stars?

Do we not hear the voices of the vastness in all of nature? Perhaps only in the measures and moments of hibernation. In our wintering. When we re-meet as strangers, at the thresholds, where the river bends beyond the lands called Hibernia and Caledonia. We winter by the hardening feet.

Healing everward.

"Affirmation relies on an other. Alignment springs from no other, no other than you."

- W.G. Kirst

Utilize the following pages to reflect on what may have come up for you as you read through the poems of this collection.

The generosity of the blank page can be an invitation, much like an ellipsis.

Reflect: What arises in you as you danced with the stanzas of EVERWARD?

Listen: What does your EVERWARD sound like when you get quiet and listen inward?

Look: What does your EVERWARD look like when you close your eyes and let them rest?

About the Author:

W.G. Kirst lives in the Pacific Northwest where he works as a technology leader guiding others through change with his gifts of empathy, compassion and creativity.

He hosts The Coffee & Change Podcast which can be found anywhere you find podcasts or streamed directly from the website: www.coffeeandchange.co

Follow the evolution of EVERWARD on Instagram & Threads: @journeyeverward

To connect and learn more about the author visit: www.journeyeverward.com

Share any reflections, reviews, feedback, insights, unveilings and re-memberings that may arise while sitting with this collection: begin@journeyeverward.com

EVERWARD

Cover illustration: "Journey Everward" by Rachel Murphy

Learn more about the author's journey at: www.journeyeverward.com

everward

A

POETRY

COLLECTION

W.G. KIRST

Enjoyed the collection?
Support the author by leaving a review on
Amazon and Goodreads.

THANK YOU!

Made in the USA
Las Vegas, NV
08 August 2024

93555075R00052